THE ARTS AND CRAFTS GARDEN

Sarah Rutherford

SHIRE PUBLICATIONS

Published in Great Britain in 2018 by Shire Publications
part of Bloomsbury Publishing Plc
PO Box 883, Oxford OX1 9PL, United Kingdom
1385 Broadway, 5th Floor, New York, NY 10018, USA
Email: shire@shirebooks.co.uk   www.shirebooks.co.uk

© 2013 Sarah Rutherford.
First published 2013; reprinted 2016 and 2018.

A CIP catalogue record for this book is available from
the British Library.

Shire Library no. 771   •   ISBN-13: 978 0 74781 298 2

Sarah Rutherford has asserted her right under the
Copyright, Designs and Patents Act, 1988, to be
identified as the author of this book.

Designed by Tony Truscott Designs, Sussex, UK
Typeset in Perpetua and Gill Sans.
Printed in China through World Print Ltd.

18 19 20   11 10 9 8 7 6 5 4 3

COVER IMAGE
The spirit of the Arts and Crafts garden is encapsulated in
George Elgood's view of Raunscliffe Hall, Leicestershire
(*The Studio*, 1908).

TITLE PAGE IMAGE
Cottage garden plants were embraced in the Arts
and Crafts garden: hollyhocks and Shirley poppies in
box-edged borders at Kellie Castle, Fife (Lorimer's first
garden), with roses for which the garden was famed. Miss
Jekyll approved and was impressed by the hollyhocks in
'big free groups'.

CONTENTS PAGE IMAGE
Intimate garden 'rooms' epitomised Arts and Crafts
gardens. This design is from one of the earliest manuals on
Arts and Crafts garden design, J. D. Sedding's *Garden-Craft
Old and New* (1891).

ACKNOWLEDGEMENTS
I would particularly like to thank Janette Ray, who
suggested the idea for the book, Mavis Batey, Jonathan
Lovie and Michael Tooley for expert advice and kind
encouragement (although any errors remaining are
of course my own), and Rosemary Jury for unfailing
encouragement and patience on jolly trips to Arts and
Crafts gardens. Philip Norman at the Garden Museum has
been of particular help in supplying engaging and unusual
images and the Landmark Trust for allowing access to
Goddards, Surrey.
The author wishes to thank the following for permission to
reproduce the following illustrations:
Alamy, page 49 (bottom), Alamy/National Trust, pages
8–9, 14, 45, 48 (bottom), 65 (both), 79; Eileen Boal, page
56 (bottom); David Bourne, page 64; The Bridgeman Art
Library, page 16 (top); C. S. Cameron, pages 39 (bottom),
41, 59; Country Life, pages 12, 68 (top); The Garden
Museum, pages 11, 16 (bottom), 22 (top), 28 (top),
51 (centre, bottom), 66, 69 (all), 70 (both); Lindsay
Garnock-Jones, page 26; Pete Hackney, page 28 (bottom);
Hestercombe Gardens Trust, pages 18 (bottom), 19, 24,
48 (top), 62; John Leverton, page 51 (top); Jonathan
Lovie, page 38; National Trust/The Bridgeman Art
Library, page 45; Teena Vallerine, page 37;
Nick Wood/Lakeland Arts, page 7 (bottom).
All other images are from the author's collection.

Shire Publications is supporting the Woodland Trust, the UK's leading woodland conservation charity, by funding the dedication of trees.

CONTENTS

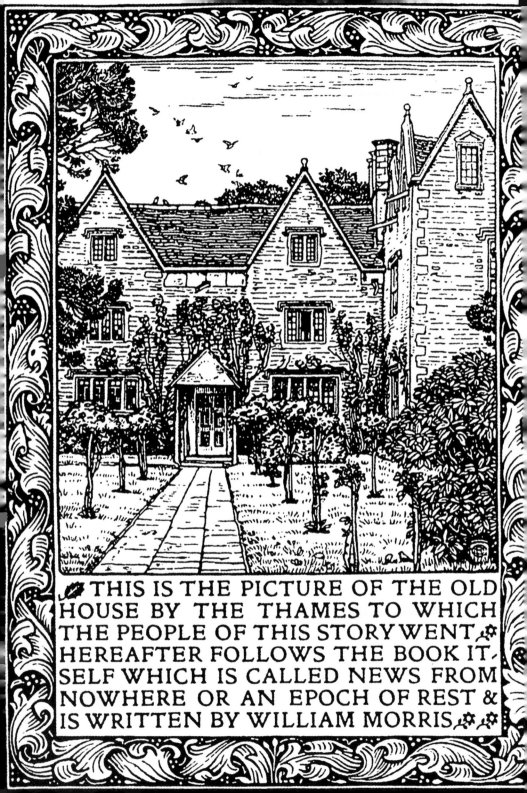

THIS IS THE PICTURE OF THE OLD
HOUSE BY THE THAMES TO WHICH
THE PEOPLE OF THIS STORY WENT
HEREAFTER FOLLOWS THE BOOK IT·
SELF WHICH IS CALLED NEWS FROM
NOWHERE OR AN EPOCH OF REST &
IS WRITTEN BY WILLIAM MORRIS

INTRODUCTION: THE ARTS AND CRAFTS MOVEMENT

THE ARTS AND CRAFTS MOVEMENT is best known as an international design movement, but it also embodied a moral code and whole way of life for its greatest enthusiasts. It flourished in the late nineteenth century, with its greatest popularity in the first years of the twentieth century. A reverence for nature and for the traditions of building and craftsmanship were fundamental to its values. Its influence has continued and is still felt today. The foundations of its craft and design philosophy, which embodied a strong social and moral core, were laid by the Pre-Raphaelite artistic movement from the 1850s, and strengthened by the Artworkers' Guild from its foundation in 1884. A number of personalities are inextricably bound up in its genesis, development and enthusiastic acceptance as a way of life.

Initially the Arts and Crafts Movement was led by the writer, designer and socialist William Morris (1834–96) and the architect Charles Voysey (1857–1941). The movement was inspired by the writings of John Ruskin and the designs and ideas of the architect and designer A. W. N. Pugin, who saw a strong relationship between architecture, design and the crafts, and emphasised nature as a source of inspiration. These ideals were largely a reaction against the impoverished state of the decorative arts at the time: shoddy, mass-produced objects were created by machine operators in appalling conditions. Instead the movement embraced the return to the ideals of simplicity, utility, craftsmanship, natural materials and vernacular forms for which Morris so passionately argued, produced with dignity of labour.

William Morris was an influential friend of the Pre-Raphaelites. This group of avant-garde painters associated with John Ruskin arose in the 1850s as a loose association of like-minded artists; leading lights included William Holman Hunt, John Everett Millais, Dante Gabriel Rossetti and Edward Burne-Jones. In their approach they were greatly influenced by nature, detailing the natural world in their work with bright, sharply focused techniques. Alongside this Morris made his name as an artist and manufacturer of high-quality, well-designed furnishings and as a socialist writer. He was also a pioneer of conservation practices and principles that underpin today's

Opposite:
The Arts and Crafts ideal: Kelmscott Manor as portrayed for Morris's idealistic socialist novel *News from Nowhere*, published by his Kelmscott Press (1893).

conservation movement, and he founded the Society for the Protection of Ancient Buildings in 1877. As a key part of the Arts and Crafts Movement he helped to found the Artworkers' Guild, whose members expressed the principles of the movement in their high-quality craftsmanship and design, and in his writing set out the origins of ideas that were so influential in the development of gardens.

The Arts and Crafts Movement turned its back on the artificiality and intensive manufacture represented by the High Victorian industrial world and instead applied medieval, romantic or folk styles of decoration. Followers espoused an idealised way of living which influenced all aspects of the home: the house, its furnishings and decoration, textiles, fine arts and jewellery, books, and of course its setting: the garden. Throughout this, the representation of nature continued to be a seminal motif.

William Morris (1834–96), co-founder of the Arts and Crafts Movement in the 1860s. Relief by George Jack (1902) on the Memorial Cottages, Kelmscott, designed by Philip Webb.

In 1899 the Scots architect Robert Lorimer summed up the ethos of the Arts and Crafts garden in the *Architectural Review*, when he described his ideal:

A garden that is in tune with the house, a garden that has a quite different sort of charm from the park outside, a garden that is an intentional and deliberate piece of careful design, a place that is garnished and nurtured with the tenderest care, but which becomes less trim as it gets further from the house, and then naturally and gradually marries with the demesne that lies beyond ... you can stroll right out into the garden inclosed ... but what a paradise can such a place be made! Such surprises – little gardens within the garden, the month's garden, the herb garden, the yew alley. The kitchen garden too, and this nothing to be ashamed of, to be smothered away far from the house, but made delightful by its laying out. Great intersecting walks of shaven grass, on either side borders of the brightest flowers backed up by low espaliers hanging with shining apples.

A rich Arts and Crafts interior embodied the warmth and fellowship of the Arts and Crafts Movement. Falkewood, by the major architect of the movement, M. H. Baillie Scott (1906).

The most highly regarded Arts and Crafts homes were planned as an entirety. The garden was an extension of the house, an integral part of the whole home intended to embody the Arts and Crafts principles. Those Arts and Crafts homes regarded as the most successful united the house, its decor and contents, and setting.

Philip Webb (1831–1915) was Morris's friend and a pioneer Arts and Crafts architect who became revered for his approach, as well as a fellow conservationist. In 1859, when they were both young, idealistic men, Webb designed Morris's first house, Red House, from scratch in an orchard in rural Bexleyheath, then just beyond south-east London near the medieval Pilgrims' Route to Canterbury. Morris's Red House has been described as the

Interiors were also light and airy. The White Drawing Room, Blackwell, Cumbria, designed by M. H. Baillie Scott (1898–1900).

Red House, Bexleyheath, Kent, by Philip Webb (1859). This was William Morris's Pre-Raphaelite family home, based on a romantic medieval lifestyle, uniting the house and garden.

architectural Arts and Crafts springboard, as it heralded Arts and Crafts principles. However, the garden was more Pre-Raphaelite than Arts and Crafts, emphasising the value of detail without the strong unity of design that defines the latter (and later) movement. Even so, it was certainly a forerunner of the Arts and Crafts garden.

At Red House a group of small, medieval-style gardens enclosed by rustic fences and trellis was sprinkled around the house, within the esteemed traditional orchard of mixed fruit. This evoked Morris's idealised medieval world with which he imbued the exterior of the house, and its interior in

both décor and furnishing. Plants clothed Morris's romantic vision, with many flowering creepers against the walls of the house, and climbing roses over the fences of the herber-type garden compartments. His garden was 'vividly picturesque and uniquely original', with sweetbriars, orchard walks and gnarled old fruit trees. Midsummer lilies and autumn sunflowers grew in richly flowered square garden plots enclosed by 'wattled rose-trellises'.

Morris's garden ideas were later codified by the architect J. D. Sedding in his book *Garden-Craft Old and New* (1891), in which he gently criticises this approach: 'We go about in a sort of pre-Raphaelite frame of mind, where

each seemly and beauteous feature has so much to say for itself that, in the delightfulness of the details, we are apt to forget that it is the first business of any work of Art to be a unit.' Sedding was a professional designer who knew how to unite these disparate Pre-Raphaelite elements into a pleasing garden reflecting Arts and Crafts ideals.

Morris and his family left Red House after only five years, disillusioned after experimenting with an idealised but impossibly romantic dream life. Morris, his family and Rossetti in 1871 leased Kelmscott Manor, a genuinely historic manor house in deepest south-west Oxfordshire, as a country retreat. This became Morris's spiritual home, about which he wrote with fervour, particularly in his utopian *News from Nowhere* (1890), with the 1893 Kelmscott Press edition frontispiece a woodcut of the manor and its simple front garden. Kelmscott symbolised the style of life Morris wished to be available to all, and was his archetypal home, the place that time forgot.

Although the Pre-Raphaelites espoused the medieval and Gothic, when they looked to history for garden precedents no medieval gardens had survived. Instead, the nearest thing to them, and handily one which was very attractive and at a relatively intimate scale, was the walled and terraced Renaissance enclosures of Elizabethan and Stuart manor gardens with their sundials, topiary, formal

Opposite: Kelmscott Manor, deep in the Cotswolds, the epicentre for Morris's idealised Arts and Crafts lifestyle. His family lived in this modest manor house from 1871 for sixty-seven years.

The Best Garden, Chastleton House, Oxfordshire, a type of Jacobean manor house garden idealised by Arts and Crafts designers.

Gertrude Jekyll (1843–1932), one of the greatest Arts and Crafts designers. She lived the lifestyle wholeheartedly at Munstead Wood, Surrey, built for her by her young friend Edwin Lutyens in the 1890s.

pools and gently coloured, largely native planting. This was the antithesis of high Victorian artificiality in garden design and planting. Archetypes for these included the early seventeenth-century Chastleton, Oxfordshire, and the revered Penshurst Place, Kent. Particularly well publicised was Montacute, Somerset, drawn by Inigo Triggs and published in his *Formal Gardens in England and Scotland* (1902), including the two massive square summerhouses in the forecourt. In Scotland the indigenous equivalent, the tower house-cum-castle garden, formed the model, and was particularly promoted by Robert Lorimer.

Gertrude Jekyll (1843–1932) was the other key figure in the Arts and Crafts Movement. She was an artist, craftswoman, suffragist, and, most famously, a garden designer, who embraced the Arts and Crafts philosophy early on. In 1900 she wrote, 'if I may give myself a title so honourable [as a] garden artist'. Like Morris, Miss Jekyll lived this philosophy wholeheartedly, not just as a hobby. Along with Morris and Voysey, she was one of its most influential champions. She visited Morris's display of craftsmanship at the 1862 International Exhibition in London and paid tribute to his enormous influence on public taste, and met him in 1868. She urged the preservation of the old craft material being discarded in her beloved West Surrey. She more than anyone else brought gardening into Arts and Crafts, especially when she became gardens adviser to the magazine *Country Life Illustrated* after it appeared in 1897, itself a key promoter of Arts and Crafts ideals under its owner and proprietor Edward Hudson.

Miss Jekyll contributed designs to over four hundred gardens in Britain and Ireland, Europe and the United States. She was perhaps the greatest influence on the architect Edwin Lutyens (1869–1944), who, under her direction early on in his career, in 1896 designed her home, Munstead Wood (Surrey), for her to live out her Arts and Crafts principles, one of more than six hundred commissions in his own career.

In and around Surrey Jekyll and Lutyens were at the epicentre of the movement, at its zenith between *c.* 1885 and 1914. But the movement was influential in gardens throughout Britain, Ireland, and abroad. In England concentrations of gardens grew up in the Cotswolds, including a fashionable American set in Broadway and a more self-effacing group with simpler tastes around Sapperton, and also in the Lake District, East Anglia and the Southwest. In Scotland examples were more scattered.

The movement influenced the contemporary Garden Cities espoused initially by social reformer Ebenezer Howard (1850–1928), moving the ideals from the wealthy few to the masses. Smaller houses were grouped at a large scale, all with their own gardens linked by coherent town planning and high-quality public open spaces. Ebenezer Howard and his followers believed that living in a spacious and well-built environment could only improve people's health and welfare and that such environments required careful thought and planning. Howard expressed his views in his influential *Garden Cities of Tomorrow* (1902). As well as commissioning designs for communal public areas such as parks and civic spaces, they commissioned attractive and varied houses on a modest scale from some of the best architects of the day, including Arts and Crafts adherents. These communities had management trusts, which ensured that the visual unity was preserved, and most survive to be visited today. Garden Cities, villages and suburbs following this model were founded in the late nineteenth and early twentieth centuries, including Lever Brothers' Port Sunlight, near Birkenhead on the Wirral peninsula (founded in 1888), Cadburys' Bournville in Birmingham (begun in the 1890s), Letchworth Garden City, Hertfordshire, where Howard's principles were taken most seriously (founded in 1903), and Hampstead Garden Suburb, London (begun in 1907).

The Garden City Movement translated the ideals of the Arts and Crafts from the wealthy cognoscenti to improve the lives of the less affluent. Letchworth Garden City expressed Ebenezer Howard's vision of well-designed homes and attractive surroundings for all.

DESIGN AND DESIGNERS

THE ARTS AND CRAFTS GARDEN did more than just reflect a superficial fashion in design. It reflected contemporary social and cultural values in reaction to High Victorian artificiality in gardens. In doing so it blazed a trail in garden design which is still strongly felt today. It also rooted the whole site firmly in its locality using topography, and indigenous materials and styles where possible.

In England the style took the rural manor house garden and combined this framework with an updated version of cottage gardening, idealised in the picturesque cottage gardens painted by Gertrude Jekyll's friend Helen Allingham (1848–1926), Kate Greenaway and others. This underpinned the resultant series of 'garden rooms', filled with topiary and billowing borders, and given structure and character using local materials and craftsmanship. Usually the garden complemented a genuinely historic manor house (Snowshill Manor, Gloucestershire), or a modern house trying to be one (Home Place/Voewood, Norfolk), or else an overgrown new or extended would-be cottage (Munstead Wood, Surrey) of a type requisitioned by the affluent middle classes. The style was also used for a few institutions, including the King Edward VII Sanatorium, Midhurst, West Sussex (1903–8, one of Miss Jekyll's most extensive garden commissions), and other public sites such as communal gardens, including Waterlow Court, Hampstead Garden Suburb, and commemorative sites including the Compton Cemetery and the Phillips Memorial Garden at Godalming, Surrey.

Architecture was central to the Arts and Crafts Movement. In the garden the house was the focal point, but the design embraced other buildings too. The garden was supposed to surround the house, with the flower garden overlooked by the main family rooms, usually south-facing if possible, and the forecourt on the rear, north side, where the drive led in from the road. The house was best set off by being presented on a formal terrace. The planting was essential to clothe and soften this formal structure in exuberant or subtle manner. Sensitive use of local materials and techniques and the inherent craftsmanship were key. Of all the Arts and Crafts architects in England perhaps Charles Voysey, Edwin Lutyens and Mackay Hugh Baillie Scott were the most successful in creating the

Opposite:
M. H. Baillie Scott's formal garden layout (c. 1920) at Snowshill Manor, Gloucestershire, was a seamless extension of the house, softened by billowing planting.

15

An idealised
country cottage:
Rose Cottage,
Shottermill,
painted by
Helen Allingham,
the best-known
of the artists who
encouraged a
nostalgia for
romanticised
cottages and
gardens evoked
by Arts and Crafts
designers.

Home Place
(now Voewood),
Holt, Norfolk,
where E. S. Prior
united the design
and fabric of the
house and garden
(1903–6).

epitome of the English country home, combining both its house and garden
and rooting them firmly in the locality.

In Scotland the model for the layout was usually a Scottish tower house,
essentially a small castle. Robert Lorimer produced the best-known Arts and
Crafts gardens of this type, most notably at Earlshall, Fife, in the 1890s, as

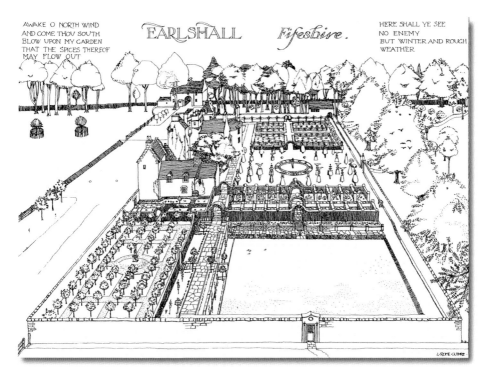

AWAKE O NORTH WIND
AND COME THOU SOUTH
BLOW UPON MY GARDEN
THAT THE SPICES THEREOF
MAY FLOW OUT

EARLSHALL   *Fifeshire.*

HERE SHALL YE SEE
NO ENEMY
BUT WINTER AND ROUGH
WEATHER

did Robert Weir Schultz. Earlshall was admired by Gertrude Jekyll and was, perhaps, one of the most important gardens to twentieth-century gardeners, influencing the designs of great gardens including Sissinghurst Castle (Kent), Crathes Castle (Aberdeenshire), and Hidcote Manor (Gloucestershire). The Scots approach, rather than evoking cottages and manor houses, was rooted in traditional Scottish castle gardens, contrasting, as Lorimer said, 'The natural park up to the walls of the house on the one [exposed] side, on the other you stroll right out into the garden inclosed [on the sheltered side]; but what a paradise can such a place be made'. The garden was revealed sequentially, always inviting further exploration.

The Arts and Crafts garden style was a romantic construct of what a country manor house or castle garden should have been. It is loosely defined by a combination of formal terraces and walls and precisely clipped hedges, softened by billowing planting of bulbs, herbaceous plants, shrubs, climbers and annuals, and punctuated by gazebos, gateways, sundials, pergolas and chess boards or menageries of topiary. All this was laid out on an intimate, human scale, with many surprises and humorous touches, and was very pleasing to inhabit. Not every area was formally drawn, with more distant areas dissolving into swelling flowering shrubberies and winding grass

Robert Lorimer's Earlshall Castle, Fife (1891–1900), was one of the most important gardens to twentieth-century design: compartmentalised, and inspired by seventeenth-century enclosed Scottish castle gardens, it was admired by Gertrude Jekyll.

17

Right: Edwin
Lutyens united
his house and
garden for Edward
Hudson, which was
clothed with plants
by Gertrude Jekyll.
Deanery Garden,
Sonning, Berkshire
(1899–1901).

Below:
Hestercombe,
Somerset
(1903–9), a great
work of the most
celebrated and
prolific Arts and
Crafts garden
partnership:
architect
Edwin Lutyens
and plantswoman
Gertrude Jekyll.

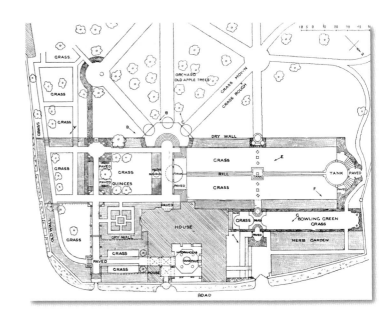

paths (in the manner prescribed by William Robinson in his seminal book promoting more naturalistic styles, *The Wild Garden*, 1870), with views into the distant, unspoilt countryside. This became a fundamental principle, as expressed by the designer Thomas Mawson: 'the further we proceed from the house the freer should be the treatment of the details of the garden scheme,' echoing the views expressed in Robinson's first edition of *The English Flower Garden* (1883), to which Miss Jekyll contributed.

WHAT MAKES AN ARTS AND CRAFTS GARDEN?

It is difficult to define an Arts and Crafts garden absolutely. It is an elusive style, but a typical example usually has a large proportion of the following; other contemporary gardens may have some or all of these, but not in the Arts and Crafts spirit.

DESIGN

Layout: formal forecourt, flower and paved gardens, herbaceous borders, hedges, kitchen garden, orchard, nuttery, tennis courts and croquet lawns, shrubberies, sometimes parkland.

Typical stone
terrace walls
and flights of
steps formalising
garden slopes.
M. H. Baillie Scott's
St Catherine's
Court, Bath
(*Houses and
Gardens*, 1906).

A family garden,
designed by
Thomas Mawson
for his brother,
nurseryman
Robert Mawson.
Shrublands,
Windermere
(1907).

Enclosures: a feeling of intimacy from small-scale spaces in a garden of rooms, anticipating surprises always just around the corner. Enclosures were formal around the house, with the lines softening further away into wooded glades and shrubberies.

Changes of level: these added greatly to the interest and were fully exploited to make the most of the topography.

Complexity of design: a skilful combination of symmetry, axes and vistas to make the garden seem larger and draw in the surrounding setting.

Views: the rural setting was often embraced in views beyond the garden, the more extensive the better. Sometimes a small park was laid out around the garden. Formal vistas through the garden were framed by clipped hedges.

STRUCTURES

Styles: historic styles of the Renaissance were evoked, particularly late Tudor and Stuart; also the vernacular and rustic, combined with originality and flair to create a coherent and inviting composition.

Craftsman construction: demonstrating the creative use of traditional materials and methods.

The house: this was the heart of the garden, with integral linking devices such as loggias and deep porches.

Materials: mellow local materials, rooted in the locale, preferably with the patina of age, with a reliance on honest craftsmanship. Stone was best for walls, or roughcast finish, with hefty structural timbers emphasised, preferably in bare oak, and roofs of handmade clay tiles or stone slates.

Garden walls, steps, paving and terraces: in local materials defining the enclosures and dealing with changes in level. They most strongly defined the garden of rooms, with walls either used as prominent backdrops or smothered in climbers.

Ornamental structures: pergolas, loggias, gazebos, dovecotes, well heads, formal pools and stone-lined rills, fountains, sundials, pots, staddle stones, sculpture.

PLANTING

Old-fashioned flowers, traditional trees, and vegetable gardens of the cottage garden; these were used with recent introductions in the herbaceous border (known in the 1880s as 'the hardy flower border') and rose and shrub gardens. The floral acme was a combination of roses, lilies, flowering climbers and herbaceous borders.

Freedom of growth in borders; informal massing.

Soft mellow colours, often contrasting with hot colours. In Miss Jekyll's borders the hot scarlets, reds and oranges of hardy and half-hardy perennials, biennials and annuals (e.g. *Kniphofia*, *Dahlia* 'Fire King' and 'Cochineal',

Gertrude Jekyll's apparently artless combination of shapes and colours was expertly designed to appear uncontrived. June borders, Munstead Wood, Surrey (*Gardens for Small Country Houses*, 1912).

An idealised combination of freedom of growth, soft colours, informal massing, and climbers smothering pergolas, reined in by the formal lines of paving, pergola columns and pool (M. H. Baillie Scott, *Houses and Gardens*, 1906).

Canna, Monarda, Gladiolus × *brenchleyensis, Salvia* and *Pelargonium*) were flanked by soft, mellow yellows, greys, purples and blues.

Climbers freely smothering pergolas and swags, romped up walls, and spilling out over the formal structures.

Closely clipped hedges, which defined 'rooms', framed vistas in and beyond
the garden and confined the luxuriant planting.

Witty and detailed topiary populating the 'rooms' with characteristic
ornamental shapes (chessmen, birds and animals, geometric shapes)
while giving structure and form.

RODMARTON MANOR

Rodmarton Manor, Gloucestershire, embodies the key elements of the Arts and Crafts home: building, interior, furnishings and garden were created as an ensemble over twenty years from 1909; this is all the more important as it remains intact in the ownership of the original family, the Biddulphs. Its layout is typical: formal garden rooms around the house are defined by clipped hedges and dry stone walls, becoming less formal and more mysterious further away, with a breathtaking view over the ha-ha to the hazy Marlborough Downs some seventeen miles away. It had the traditional kitchen garden but also three up-to-date lawn tennis courts, enclosed by clipped yew hedges.

Cooler colours of green foliage, lawn and masonry were valued alongside colourful floral displays. The busy Troughery at Rodmarton is calmed and united by the shades of pleached limes, lawn, topiary and dry-stone walls.

The formal rill was a trademark of Edwin Lutyens, here planted by Miss Jekyll with water-loving irises. Hestercombe, Somerset (1904–6).

DESIGNERS

Designers were driven by their passion for the movement to communicate its benefits. J. D. Sedding published one of the first Arts and Crafts garden design manuals, *Garden-Craft Old and New* (1891). He was heavily influenced by Morris, ensuring that their influence on the next generation of architects was considerable. Sedding managed to bridge the divide between the architects,

such as Reginald Blomfield, who believed that a garden was essentially an architectural construct, and the gardeners, such as William Robinson, who believed that as important, if not more so, to garden design were the planting and gardening skills. At opposite ends of the design spectrum are Blomfield's *The Formal Garden in England* (1892) and Robinson's *The Wild Garden* (1870 and many later editions), *The English Flower Garden* (1883) and his other books about naturalistic planting; paradoxically, both authors became key influences on Arts and Crafts designers.

Such seemingly opposite opinions were harmoniously united to great effect in the partnership of architect Edwin Lutyens and his mentor: plantswoman, designer and deeply committed Arts and Crafts aficionado Gertrude Jekyll. Together they produced dozens of acclaimed gardens from the 1890s into the 1930s. Lutyens's houses and garden layouts were published at the time by *Country Life* and brought together in *Small Country Houses of Today* (1910) and *Houses and Gardens by E. L. Lutyens* (1913), while Miss Jekyll herself wrote prolifically on gardens and gardening, with well over a thousand articles for Robinson's horticultural magazines (*The Garden*, *Gardening Illustrated*), *Country Life* and other periodicals, and fifteen books, including *Gardens for Small Country Houses* (1912) and *Garden Ornament* (1918), which were influential design and pattern books covering features that were ideal for Arts and Crafts admirers.

The most successful garden designers were Arts and Crafts architects who often worked with plantsmen, or landscape designers, or owner amateurs inspired to respond to the genius of the place. *Country Life* and *The Studio* magazines promoted some designers and their work, particularly Lutyens and Lorimer, illustrating and explaining the houses and gardens so that they would be particularly appealing to readers.

Key architects who designed gardens included Edwin Lutyens, Robert Lorimer, Ernest Barnsley (1863–1926), Charles Voysey (1857–1941), Mackay Hugh Baillie Scott (1865–1945) and Philip Webb. Architects often worked with plantsmen in the manner of Lutyens and Jekyll, most prominent being the gardener and writer William Robinson, and the society lady Norah Lindsay. Landscape architects (then an embryo profession) such as George Dillistone (died 1957) and Thomas Mawson (1861–1933) straddled both disciplines and were able to design everything in a new garden. These designers translated the ideology of Morris and Ruskin into a sophisticated style and way of living uniting the philosophies of architects such as Blomfield and gardeners such as Robinson. Many contemporary nurserymen designed gardens and provided the plants (as did Miss Jekyll), including Backhouse, Barr & Sons, Jackmans, Paul & Son, Youell & Co., and in Scotland Cockers in Aberdeen and Watts in Cupar. A list of major designers and their key commissions is given in the Appendix.

DEFINING THE GARDEN: BOUNDARIES AND MATERIALS

IT WAS CRUCIAL to distinguish the garden from the wider setting such as the park, if any, and the countryside beyond. This helped to ensure that the garden, as Morris advised, could not be mistaken for anything else. Within the garden its various 'rooms' and vistas also needed clear definition. Walls, terraces, gates, steps and hedges were used in profusion to enclose the garden and its 'rooms' in various ways, and to screen or frame views within or beyond the garden. The choice of materials was a key aspect in establishing the character of the garden: materials had to be in harmony with their locality, preferably sourced from as close by as possible and worked in traditional ways.

Freestanding walls enclosed forecourts, kitchen gardens and ornamental gardens to create those 'rooms' reminiscent of the manor garden. Walls were usually built of the indigenous stone, whether Westmorland slate in the Lake District, Bargate stone in Surrey, Wealden stone in Sussex and Kent, or pale oolitic limestone in the Cotswolds, embedding the garden firmly in its geological origins. Where the stone could be smoothly ashlar faced, this might be used in a building to help unite the garden with the materials of the house, but often walls, particularly low ones, were built of small pieces of rubble.

Brick was used where clay prevailed over stone, such as in Berkshire, and other parts of the Home Counties including areas of Kent. Bricks were preferably hand-made and of mellow red, buff or plum colours. There were no harsh finishes or colours; sometimes more than one colour was used, but only if the result was very subtle, the idea being to emulate Tudor brickwork of the sort depicted in loving detail by Nathaniel Lloyd of Great Dixter, East Sussex, in his influential book *A History of English Brickwork* (1925).

Where the local building material was not attractive or durable enough to be left exposed it was rendered with roughcast, or 'harled' in Scotland, adding an attractive organic texture. This finish was traditional in some areas of poor stone, or where modern and cheap concrete blocks were chosen, and became a typical material of Arts and Crafts designers in areas such as Essex, the Lake District and the West Country. Concrete was used as a structural material, but not generally as a plain finish in its own right.

Opposite:
Steps directed axes linking various garden levels with the terraces around the house. Tirley Garth, Cheshire (C .E. Mallows, 1906–12).

Complex steps not only linked various levels attractively but also acted as a pivot to reach various parts of the garden. Great Dixter, East Sussex.

The great rendered wall at Blackwell, Cumbria (M. H. Baillie Scott and Thomas Mawson, c. 1900), redolent of medieval defence near the Scottish border. It dominates the lower levels of the garden, provides a surface for climbing plants, and retains a path and terrace above with panoramic views of Windermere.

Changes of level added eye-catching variety. On an elevated site, near the house or other principal building, walled terraces were preferred to deal with changes of level rather than slopes, as they established the required formality. Even on naturally level sites sunken gardens were scooped out to fulfill this need, such as at Home Place (now Voewood), Norfolk. Here E. S. Prior built and exuberantly decorated his 'butterfly' plan house with materials excavated from in front of it, and the resultant large hole became the focal sunken parterre with a terrace walk behind it.

Dry-stone walls provided texture and rhythm using local materials and patterns. At Rodmarton, Gloucestershire, a terrace wall provides a long garden bench, softened by a turf seat and self-sown plants.

Terrace walls were built of the same materials as the freestanding walls, depending on the locality. They were often given articulation with interestingly shaped buttresses and enlivened by geometric flights of steps, sometimes elaborately nonsensical, sometimes with gateways too. These walls might be several yards high, such as the rendered one below the house at Blackwell, Cumbria, making a bold statement in the design. Mostly they were lower and more self-effacing, however, sometimes only a few inches high and often of dry-stone, their texture contributing to what is now regarded as characteristic walling in an Arts and Crafts garden. Terrace walls formed a useful backdrop to herbaceous borders or lawns, or else were hidden by clipped hedges.

Elaborate timber gateways with overthrows or hoods were often used to mark pedestrian entrances off lanes and public paths (T. Mawson, *The Art and Craft of Garden Making*, 1900).

Occasionally walls were used in ha-has above key vistas against a little pseudo-park, such as at Goddards, Surrey, and Rodmarton and Hidcote, Gloucestershire. Retaining walls contributed a quiet background texture and colour and were used for standing pots on the parapet or perhaps as seats. Above them hedges were sometimes grown or paths were laid out to take advantage of the prospect.

Gates and gateways made a defining statement, setting the scene for what was to come. They linked the various garden spaces and were often treated very ornamentally. Gateways could be of similar materials to the adjacent walls, of dressed stone, or of solid timber, usually oak, either left to

weather to its mellow silver colour or painted white. The grandest gateways had overthrows or sometimes hoods. These were often set in a boundary wall, like the gateway from the lane at Morris's Kelmscott, or giving access to an intimate entrance court, such as that at Woodside, Chenies, Buckinghamshire (an early Lutyens/Jekyll commission), or a walled garden such as Peto's kitchen garden off the lane at Iford Manor. The gates themselves were of various traditional materials, but particularly favoured were oak, exposed or painted, if possible fashioned from indigenous estate timber, and wrought iron, preferably worked at a local forge into traditional patterns or natural motifs.

Clipped yew hedges were another key, almost ubiquitous, feature, but again they were not new and were much used in earlier manor house gardens. Hedges offered shelter, seclusion and well-defined spaces. They were an initially cheaper alternative to the garden wall, enclosing spaces, but when they were the usual dark evergreens they added a calm backdrop to the garden 'room' or darkly framed a vista. Native shrubs and trees offered the ideal species. Yew was the most popular hedging material as it grew relatively quickly into the required shape and height and formed a permanently dense, smooth, uniform backdrop, like a plastered and painted wall. A yew hedge could also

Wrought-iron gates, plain apart from the elaborate cresting. The White House, Helensburgh, Scotland.

An oak gateway, its great scale reminiscent of centuries of craftsmanship. R. Plumb, Napsbury Hospital, Hertfordshire (c. 1905).

accommodate topiary. At Kelmscott William Morris clipped the top of a large hedge into the shape of Sigurd's dragon Fafnir, a character in *Sigurd the Volsung* (1876), which he felt was his best work. Other, more conventional animals or geometric shapes might sprout above the level top such as the peacocks at Rodmarton or chessmen.

Box, although valued and often used for its similarly uniform surface, was much slower to grow in the first place; holly, with its less uniform, crinkly surface, and other evergreens were also used as long as they responded tamely to clipping, but they never quite lived up to the qualities of yew. A few deciduous plants were used, particularly the traditional beech and hornbeam,

Clipped yew hedges and topiary-framed garden rooms and key views. Rodmarton, Gloucestershire.

which, when clipped as hedging, retain their leaves for much of the winter. But the labour required to keep a clipped hedge to shape and size was prodigious. However ruthless the gardener in clipping hedges, they always outgrew their intended size over the years, sometimes squeezing the garden 'room' down to merely a tiny cupboard. Sometimes dwarf box hedges formally enclosed beds against paths and paving, the hedge kept to a few inches high and wide while the planting within grew exuberantly. Limes and other deciduous trees were pleached to form 'stilt-hedges' alongside walks, such as at Hidcote and Sissinghurst, or above terrace walls, lifting the body

Paving was important to design as well as structure. Local materials were preferred, sometimes in great variety, patterned to vary texture and colour (T. Mawson, *The Art and Craft of Garden Making*, 1900).

PAVED GARDEN WALK LEADING TO SUMMER HOUSE

of the hedge above the clear trunks below, which acted as a formal columned feature allowing views out of the walk.

Paths and paving helped to define the character of a particular part of the garden. In formal enclosures paths were generally straight, but further from the house they might become sinuous routes into the unknown hinterland. Paving materials were generally grass, rolled gravel, local stone slabs (squared or in irregular shapes as crazy paving), or a mixture of many of these in various parts of the garden. The paving pattern was sometimes part of the ornament. Lutyens was the master of creativity in paving, using an imaginative range of materials beyond the usual, including millstones, tile-on-edge and brick-on-edge together in complex patterns. Others also used imaginative schemes, such as Mawson and Baillie Scott. Circular or semicircular steps were a speciality of Lutyens, often using a concave flight above one or more convex flights, or using a millstone to turn an angle. The path material often defined the character of a particular area, with formal stone paths near the house, often extended to surface a whole terrace, and gravel or rubble stone or grass paths used further away.

The walled garden, Hampton Manor, Warwickshire. Its fine walls and gateways were designed by Thomas Mawson around 1900, including this Jacobean-style gateway.

GARDEN BUILDINGS

THE HOUSE was the focus of the garden design and views, but since time immemorial garden buildings added variety and structure for those who could afford them. Garden buildings offered shelter from the elements, shade in summer and a place to retreat to from the hubbub, to commune with controlled nature. Some buildings performed other useful functions. Arts and Crafts garden buildings were no different: they added interest and substance

A genuinely old pavilion at Morris's Kelmscott has the timeless antiquity and connection with its locality that was integral to Arts and Crafts ideals.

to the garden, enlivened the garden 'rooms', terminated vistas and provided places for quiet contemplation and enjoying the prospect across the garden or the wider landscape. Depending on the wealth of the owner, they could be large and elaborate or modest and relatively cheap, but in either case many were used as an opportunity for a virtuoso display of craftsmanship in the ornamental use of materials.

Traditional materials were de rigueur, particularly in roofing, where cheap thatch, and tiles of local stone or clay were materials of choice. Lead rainwater goods were preferred to modern cast iron as being traditional (but expensive), and sometimes lead was worked into elaborate patterns. Outstanding examples include the straps supporting downpipes and hoppers at Rodmarton Manor, Gloucestershire, bearing vignettes of flowers and animals in relief, including monkeys, owls and robins, designed by Norman Jewson, *c.* 1913. At Goddards, Surrey, Lutyens's ornate lead downpipe from the roof feeds the tall, slender rainwater barrel in the Well Court.

Some garden structures were integral to the house, such as courtyard loggias and porches. These of all garden buildings most obviously united the

A covered cloister or arcade enclosed by the house is a true outdoor room. Tirley Garth, Cheshire (C. E. Mallows, 1906–12).

house and garden as living spaces, as a transition between the two. This had been the intention at Red House for Morris, where deep porches with seats linked the outdoors and indoors, offering shelter in inclement weather but also fresh air and intimacy with the garden, which was heavily replicated indoors in the décor of the rooms and furnishings. Mallows's modest detached house, Three Gables, Biddenham, Bedford (1900–1), had an oversailing upper floor which was used as the roof of a verandah supported by timber poles, with a 'Peacock' seat made by J. P. White using a common Arts and Crafts motif.

A loggia is a covered cloister or arcade, open to the side, often attached to the house, but sometimes freestanding. Courtyards with loggias enclosed within the house were ideal to link house and garden and were a typical feature of grander Arts and Crafts houses. At Tirley Garth, Mallows

BUTTERFLY HOUSES AND GARDENS

The so-called 'butterfly house' was the most distinctive of the Arts and Crafts houses. During the 1890s several Arts and Crafts architects felt an urge to plan a house in the shape of a butterfly. This allowed many rooms to have many windows. It also increased the number of rooms benefiting from a southerly aspect, sheltered and warmed by the southerly wings. This plan form became popular for many types of building and persisted until after the First World War. Butterfly houses tended to use local materials, found close at hand, in an eclectic manner, with garden layouts that responded to their unusual plan form. The south-facing wings of the butterfly enclosed a particularly clement area in which terraces and lawn were laid out.

E. S. Prior produced early designs and examples: first a modest house called The Barn, Exmouth (1896–7), and later the exuberantly patterned Home Place (now called Voewood), Holt, Norfolk (1903–6), with a large formal sunken garden, kitchen garden and orchard. Prior's plan for Home Place garden, published in 1906 (*Architectural Review*), expressed his principles in the art of garden making. He preferred formal garden design for smaller plots, with native plants and trees rather than exotic species. Here he took his passion for local building materials to the extreme: the stone and flint used for building and decorating the house and garden walls was excavated from in front of the house to a depth of 6 feet, which allowed for the creation of the sunken garden. Although the terrace was a 'veritable suntrap', the house was unbearably draughty in winter and had to be modified internally.

Other major Arts and Crafts architects weighed in. Detmar Blow designed Happisburgh Manor, Norfolk (1900), with a complex compartmented garden around the house, linking it with two other houses he built, including a gatehouse. Nearby Papillon Hall was remodelled by Lutyens (1902); a substantial house was built at How Green, Hever, Kent, by Robert Weir Schultz (1910); back in Norfolk, E. B. Maufe built Kelling Hall (1912–13), while around the same time surrounded the eponymous 'garth' (or courtyard) with a low loggia with broad dressed-stone arches. From the openings at the centre of each side, semicircular steps lead down to the circular central pool. The doorway from the forecourt opens into this loggia, so that in very sunny or inclement weather the main house can be entered without exposure to the elements; in warm weather the central space is used, and the focal, stepped pool and paved courtyard are an integral part of the house. Similar loggias were designed elsewhere, including one for a house called Everdene by Baillie Scott, and at Lutyens's Folly Farm, Berkshire.

Two large, freestanding rustic thatched loggias were erected at Tylney Hall, Hampshire (Robert Weir Schultz, *c.* 1901–4), at either end of a broad path lined by borders. A freestanding brick loggia, perhaps more of a cloister given the setting, was built at Compton Cemetery, near Godalming, by the

J. L. Ball built Furze Hill (now called Foxhill) near Willersey, Gloucestershire, on a 'double suntrap plan' – he took pride in the fact that not a single room faced north.

Below: Home Place (now called Voewood) is a 'butterfly house' (E. S. Prior, 1904–6). It embraces a large terrace and sunken garden beyond, all using materials obtained on site, so that the house and garden could hardly be more closely linked.

Below:
Thomas Mawson's
freestanding loggia,
Leweston Manor,
Dorset (1905–10).

Opposite bottom:
Lorimer's
semicircular stone
arbour, Earlshall,
Fife (1890s),
is framed by
a crenellated
garden wall
and terminates a
formal grass walk.
The semicircular
seat forms an
accent to draw
the eye.

wife of the painter G. F. Watts in his memory. Its form was in harmony with its surroundings: it was moulded to its hillside site as its length curved with the lie of the land.

Summerhouses, also called gazebos and arbours, were garden pavilions, sometimes open at the front. They were used in various ways in the design. Some, such as the one at Rodmarton, terminated a long enclosed vista, in this case along a rustic stone-flagged path between herbaceous borders backed by yew hedges in the Long Garden. Lawrence Johnston's two summerhouses at Hidcote, Gloucestershire, with swept pyramidal roofs, frame the skyward vista part way along, above the twin Red Borders; one of these pavilions is aligned at right angles on a further great formal vista, the Long Walk. Some summerhouses stood self-effacingly to one side of a garden room, such as the sandstone summerhouse at Millmead, Surrey (Lutyens, 1904–7), open to the front and sides, with wooden columns at the corners supporting a pyramidal tiled roof. Voysey designed what Hermann Muthesius called 'diminutive rustic chalets with thatched roofs' at New Place, Surrey (*c.* 1900), one of which, with a broad, semicircular-arched open front, leant against a garden wall alongside the lawn. Nearby, a freestanding summerhouse, terminated a vista with rendered and battered buttress corners, its open front with a simple flat arch, and a conical thatched roof with a cockerel above.

Left: The Cotswold stone summer-house at Rodmarton is an iconic Arts and Crafts garden structure by Ernest Barnsley. At the end of the Long Garden, it gently terminates a long, colourful, double herbaceous border framed by dark yew hedges.

Summerhouses sometimes formed prospect towers and commanded aspect too. The thatched stone and timber-framed summerhouse at Great Rissington, Gloucestershire, marked the corner at the end of an elevated terrace, as did the stone summerhouse at Wyndcliffe Court, Monmouthshire (Eric Francis, Avray Tipping, 1922). Miss Jekyll's Thunder House at Munstead Wood, Surrey (Lutyens, 1895) is a primitive-looking Bargate stone belvedere with a pyramidal tiled roof, built into a wall at the corner of the kitchen garden next to a lane. From the upper floor of this triangular building, with large openings in two sides (the third opening to the north she had shuttered in order not to invade the privacy of her neighbour), she could watch the lightning during an electrical storm illuminating the Surrey landscape and enjoy the frisson of being close to storms without getting soaked.

Miss Jekyll's local Bargate stone Thunder House by Edwin Lutyens (1895). She could watch the lightning sheltered in this belvedere at the corner of the garden.

Well and spring houses have a long garden pedigree. In Arts and Crafts spirit the first was Webb's distinctly 'Frenchified' Well House (1859) at Red House, Bexleyheath, with its steep conical chateau-style tiled roof and muscular timbers. Miss Jekyll designed one and

Sports (particularly tennis) pavilions also received the Arts and Crafts treatment. One of two well-detailed timber pavilions at Rodmarton, Gloucestershire, where three courts were laid out.

decorated it at Phillimore's Spring near Wargrave, Berkshire, in 1870. In a continuing spirit of historical ornamentation for a functional structure, Clough Williams-Ellis designed a small, square dressed-stone well house with a stone-tiled ogee-shaped roof overlooking the informal water garden at the Cotswold Cornwell Manor, Oxfordshire (c. 1939). It evoked a simple Jacobean style.

Tennis pavilions were not usually of great architectural merit, but were built nearby to serve the by now ubiquitous lawn tennis courts. Even so, like the

The Apple Store, Earlshall, Fife, designed by Robert Lorimer in seventeenth-century style like a banqueting house, attached to the kitchen garden walls. The potting shed and other ancillary buildings are hidden behind the wall.

41

Modern utility could be a feature: at Goddards in rural west Surrey, Lutyens's motor house, with its barn-like deep roof, overhanging eaves and unpainted oak doors, is situated in a walled yard similar to a tiny farmyard.

Barns were popular, whether old or new. The large timber-clad Bothy at Tirley Garth, Cheshire, dominates the circular kitchen garden, the Round Acre, an integral part of C. E. Mallows's design (1906–12).

other garden buildings, they were attractive and well designed in the spirit of their surroundings. More functional buildings were also given due consideration including kitchen garden structures such as glasshouses, and agricultural buildings. Existing barns were especially valued. One was smartened up and

used as a shelter dominating one side of the Well Court at Cotswold Snowshill.
A more ramshackle one is seen in images of Miss Jekyll's Munstead Wood.
Lutyens's motor house and yard at Goddards, Surrey (1898–1900), was built
like a barn in a tiny, walled farmyard, albeit rather sanitised.

THE PHILLIPS MEMORIAL

An outstanding early civil memorial garden epitomises the Arts and Crafts style. The Phillips Memorial, Godalming, Surrey, commemorates the chief wireless operator on the *Titanic*, who died at his post in the disaster of 1912. Miss Jekyll was closely associated with the success of this project. The local Arts and Crafts architect Thackeray Turner (1853–1937) combined various structures around a courtyard with a central octagonal pool, all using Surrey forms and materials, as Lutyens had done at Miss Jekyll's own Munstead Wood. A freestanding cloister with tiled roof enclosed and sheltered visitors, with an arcaded brick wall holding the stone memorial plaque, and framing views over the adjacent park. She provided planting in a restrained style, including *Bergenia*, irises, evergreen shrubs and *Wisteria*.

The Phillips Memorial, Godalming, has planting designed by Miss Jekyll (1913).

ORNAMENTS

Opposite:
One of the more
spindly type of
dovecotes, timber
and thatched.
Beatrice Parsons,
Gardens of England
(1908).

O RNAMENTS added an important dimension to the garden, showing off taste and craftsmanship wherever possible. They punctuated the landscape at key points, adding an extra and sophisticated aspect to 'rooms', vistas and planting, with a variety of materials, positions and uses.

Country Life published Gertrude Jekyll's book *Garden Ornament* in 1918 as a profusely illustrated guide for garden owners and designers based on Arts and Crafts principles. In it she demonstrated how a range of garden structures and ornaments could be used to achieve the best possible effect, whether in the small garden or the grand estate. Other designers offered examples, notably Mawson's design guide *The Art and Craft of Garden Making* (published in five editions between 1900 and 1926), which illustrated features in many of his own schemes.

Below: Reflecting
pools provided
tranquillity and
could be used for
bathing. Lawrence
Johnston's Bathing
Pool garden,
Hidcote Manor,
Gloucestershire.

The pergola was a defining feature derived from Renaissance Italy: an open framework straddling a walk, on which to grow climbers. Early on in British garden designing, Francis Bacon, in his influential 1625 essay 'Of Gardens', devoted particular attention to the pergola. The pergola was generally used to cross an open area as the focal feature, or else ran in parallel to a garden wall. The form varied from spindly rustic timber structures, such as Norah Lindsay had at Sutton Courtenay, Oxfordshire, to hefty stone or brick pillars supporting solid oak cross beams, such as Mawson's great stretch of double columns at The Hill, Hampstead, for Lord Leverhulme, and Lutyens's one at Hestercombe, Somerset, along one side of the Plat. Elegant iron hoops across the path were common; a variant was

dual rows of timber poles with rope swags or chains linking them, lining the path or backing a pair of borders. It formed a shady tunnel enveloped in a bower of leaves, vines and flowers (although the flowers usually sought the sun on top of the pergola and insects tended to drop on the unwary at unexpected moments), and provided perhaps the closest encounter with nature in the garden.

Water is essential in any garden to add an extra dimension and that evocative plashing sound. Pools, fountains and ornamental wells were fairly common, but as water features were expensive to construct and maintain they were generally not extensive. Simple geometric pool shapes lent themselves ideally as the focal point of small, formal compartments around the house, defined with a stone edging or set within an entirely stone-paved terrace.

Smothered in foliage and flowers for much of the year, the pergola provided a bowered walk, remaining ornamental when the structure was exposed in the winter. Rose Court pergola, M. H. Baillie Scott, *Houses and Gardens*, 1906.

The dipping well was one of Miss Jekyll's favourite features, a good example being in the Well Court at Goddards, Surrey, where she provided rich planting amongst Lutyens's variety of colours and textures in the paving and walls. More restrained but lush planting surrounds the less prominent (although still highly detailed) working well, tucked away at the side of the house.

A lighter framework of cast iron hoops linked by wires supported climbers well but did not dominate the garden like timber or masonry (B. Parsons, *Gardens of England*, 1908).

Utilitarian elements were ornamented in the garden. Lutyens's working well at Goddards, Surrey (1898–1900), tucked away at the side of the house, has as much consideration as the main Well Court.

Semicircular pools were used against walls; more challenging was to let a circular pool into a wall with a semicircle projecting into the paving in front and a pipe spouting water through the mouth of a mask. In this case the wall was usually supported by a hemispherical backdrop to the pool. This came to be regarded as a particular trademark of Lutyens's gardens, along with stone-lined rills, such as at Deanery Garden, Sonning, Berkshire, and Hestercombe, Somerset, where rills and pools were combined.

Variety in a small space: materials, levels, textures, subtle colour variations, planted in shades of green, grey and lilac. Lutyens's Well Court at the heart of Goddards, Surrey (1898–1900).

The circular pool
in a hemispherical
recess was one
of Lutyens's
trademark
features,
associated
with his more
complex designs.
Hestercombe,
Somerset
(1904–6).

Seats came in various types. They could be conventional straight benches with arms and backs, curved or angled to fit an exedra or niche, or circular, square or octagonal to surround a tree trunk. The favoured material was

Formal pools
were popular,
framed by local
paving. The Well
Court, Snowshill,
Gloucestershire,
is overlooked
by a former barn.

timber, either exposed oak, or softwood painted white or green or stained brown or black. Timber replaced High Victorian cast-iron benches with a more natural, and more comfortable, seat.

Seat patterns were myriad. The successful manufacturer John P. White of Bedford (the Pyghtle Works) was renowned for his garden furniture, including gates and fences. Hermann Muthesius in *Das Englische Haus* (1904)

Shaped timber seats were popular ornaments (Walter Godfrey, *Gardens in the Making*, 1914).

The rose pergola, Upton Grey, Hampshire, contrasts the riot of François Juranville and May Queen ramblers with formal dwarf box hedges.

praised White for commissioning the best artists to design for him and for issuing 'tasteful catalogues' to 'make known and disseminate his artistically outstanding pieces'. Muthesius added that this assumed a 'certain standard of taste' on the part of the public.

Sundials in traditional ornamental patterns, or variants, were revived with enthusiasm. There were innumerable early models to use. The bronze dial or, less commonly, a complex armillary sphere, was usually set flat on an elaborate stone plinth. The dial could also be set vertically, high at the top of a slender stone shaft as Mawson did at Graythwaite, Cumbria. Occasionally terracotta was employed, such as the Compton Pottery offered. They generally formed the centrepiece of one of the terraces, gardens or lawns, situated at the crossing of paths.

A sundial evoking Renaissance scientific investigation. A sundial was essential and, depending on the size, was within most people's means. It could be traditional in form or a variation. Goddards, Surrey.

Sculpture showed off the taste, wealth and education of the owner. It was not often lavishly used in Arts and Crafts gardens, and was usually restricted to one or two key pieces placed at focal points around the house; larger collections could be spread throughout the garden. The extent of the use of sculpture was usually dependent upon the wealth of the owner. Traditional figures and decorative subjects were mostly favoured. Urns were common; also fountains and particularly masks. Lead was popular as a traditional material that withstood the British climate well, making it suitable for ornamented water features and troughs, and it showcased British craftsmanship. Stone and composite stone pieces, offered by firms such as James Pulham & Son, were also popular.

Pots and tubs were carefully placed in singles and groups around the house and on terraces. Terracotta and stone were common materials; sizes and patterns varied. Sometimes topiary was grown in pots. At Rodmarton a Troughery was created, in which small stone troughs from the farm, once used for animal feeding or drinking, were collected and planted with alpine and other small plants. Other traditional farm items were reused, including many staddle stones from the raised granaries that were often taken down. A notable collection of staddle stones encircles the outer arc of the forecourt at Rodmarton.

Terracotta was a cheaper alternative to lead or stone ornaments. The Potters' Arts Guild, also known as the Compton Pottery, centred on Compton, Surrey, produced a range of garden ornaments and cemetery memorials in clay. Mary Watts (wife of the celebrated

Leadwork was of the finest quality, often with great artistry in the design and ornamentation. Lead trough and mask, Misarden Park, Gloucestershire.

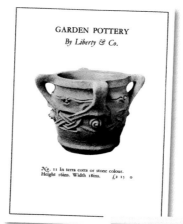

GARDEN POTTERY
By Liberty & Co.

Nọ. 11 In terra cotta or stone colour.
Height 16ins. Width 18ins.   £2 15 0

Hand-made terracotta containers were works of art but were very expensive. Liberty pot by the Compton Pottery, and Fordham topiary tub.

The "Daisy"
Box Tree Tub
～1 43/6
24" high
24" square base

painter G. F. Watts) trained locals to work red and grey terracotta clay into artistically ornamented pots, urns, sundials and seats with a strong Art Nouveau sculptural style. This was sold by the fashionable Arts and Crafts shop, Liberty's of Regent Street, London.

Animals were integral to decorative Arts and Crafts motifs from nature. In particular, birds among the boscage were key to William Morris's textile patterns, including the iconic *Strawberry Thief* wallpaper and fabric and *Woodpecker* tapestry (1885). Voysey and other designers were equally beguiled by plants, flowers, and birds such as peacocks. In the garden it was possible to keep real birds, of which ornamental doves and peacocks were most often seen and depicted; they were also represented in patterns on garden ornaments.

Peacocks added a great sense of prestige to any garden, despite the appalling racket they made at inconvenient times. They were often depicted in artistic garden scenes and formed the centrepiece of interior design motifs. They did not have

Compton Pottery terracotta garden sculpture was of the highest quality, designed and made in true Arts and Crafts spirit. Well head, Compton Cemetery, Surrey.

Troughs brought the detail of small plants closer to the eye, particularly alpines. The Troughery at Rodmarton used drinking troughs found in the fields.

specifically designed residences, being able to roost in trees. Wild birds were welcome, but the cottagers' homely hens and ducks were officially banished to the kitchen garden or remote ponds. Early in his career, in 1889, Lutyens did, however, design a whimsical, but quite solid, thatched and timber-clad Fowl House at Littleworth Cross, Surrey, for Harry Mangles.

Dovecotes were usually more modest than the great freestanding historic buildings commonly found with old manor houses such as Kelmscott. Doves, although very pretty in the garden, were a nuisance in anything more than small numbers, and as they were purely ornamental in the Arts and Crafts garden – not required for the table – they needed to be kept in check. The most elegant dovecotes were small timber pavilions perched precariously on a slender pole in which a few white doves could reside and flutter decorously around.

Some dovecotes, however, were more robust. In Sapperton, Gloucestershire, Sidney Barnsley and Ernest Gimson each built a stone dovecote in similar idiom. Each one topped a small tower above the garden wall, with tiers of holes divided by flat stones or stone slates as perches. Barnsley's one at Beechanger was circular in plan, protected from attack at the base by a ring of iron teeth hanging down over the base stone; Gimson's one at Leasowes (c. 1903) was square. Sometimes dovecotes were incorporated into other buildings in traditional manner, as Barnsley did in the apex of a garden archway at Combend Manor, Gloucestershire.

A chunky dovecote, the focus of the forecourt of the remodelled house at Little Pednor, Chartridge, Buckinghamshire (c.1910, Forbes and Tate), surrounded by staddle stones from a dismantled granary, with an unusual gateway beyond.

PLANTS AND PLANTING

ARTS AND CRAFTS PLANTING combined (but was not restricted to) herbaceous borders, hedged terraces, climbers, lawns, topiary, roses and more remote woodland gardens. But planting had its tensions. Around the house a hedonistic approach to blowsy border planting, climbers, and self-sown plants in paved terraces and walls, was held in check by the strict lines of clipped hedges, rose swags and pergolas, and populated by mannered topiary figures. Further afield things relaxed into more naturalistic woodland gardens planted with trees, shrubs and bulbs. Further tensions arose within borders where Morris's favoured, if naïve, cottage planting in unstructured colours and clumps was taken into another dimension by the designers, using sophisticated varieties and colour theories.

Talented ladies of good breeding, such as Gertrude Jekyll and Norah Lindsay, flourished in their design enterprises alongside professional landscapers who combined planting and structural design, including Thomas Mawson and George Dillistone. They wrote extensively to produce a profuse canon of planting theories.

William Robinson and Miss Jekyll were perhaps the most prolific writers on planting, and, unsurprisingly, their theories mirrored Arts and Crafts ideals. They abhorred obvious artificiality in flower borders, particularly seasonal bedding in serried ranks and eye-watering colour blocks and clashes. Instead they preferred informality of flowers, swathes of soft colours with strong highlights, defined within compartments, dissolving into softer colourful shrubberies and 'wild gardens'. Abundance in borders was key, but this resulted in the tension between native traditional flowers and cottage garden varieties, and the colour symphonies and textures orchestrated by Miss Jekyll, which aimed to appear natural but were highly contrived in terms of the colours and varieties of plants. Self-sown plants continued the theme of unstructured abundance (which also allowed the lazy gardener more latitude), especially in the cracks between terrace and path paving, softened by the flowers and airy foliage of small, harmless annuals and perennials.

Opposite:
The wild garden was important further from the house. At John Ruskin's Brantwood, Coniston, Cumbria, brightly coloured azaleas and other flowering shrubs lined the path to the lake.

The typical combination of gaily coloured, blowsy borders whose lines were restrained by contrasting dark green clipped yew hedges and populated by topiary chessmen, Compton Wynyates, Warwickshire.

One of the borders in the garden of High Glanau, Lydart, Monmouthshire (from 1923), the architect H. Avray Tipping's own house.

The severe lines
of the house,
its roughcast
elevations and
dominant red
roofs were
enlivened by
numerous small
garden features
and planting
(M. H. Baillie
Scott, Everdene).

In Scotland the reaction to High Victorian gardening was heralded by Frances Jane Hope (died 1880), whose articles in *The Gardeners' Chronicle* in the 1860s and 1870s promoted more relaxed and natural planting schemes. Miss Hope's thoughts were published posthumously in her book *Notes and Thoughts on Gardens and Woodlands* (1881), two years before Robinson's vastly popular *English Flower Garden* (1883), which includes a three-page article by her on hardy flowers.

The essence of the herbaceous border was summed up by Norah Lindsay in *Country Life* (1929): 'The secret to a successful herbaceous border is to have a profusion of hardy plants well placed in irregular groups and patches,

Planting schemes
were not all muted
shades of lilac and
grey. The recently
introduced
deciduous azaleas
were popular, as
at Tirley Garth,
Cheshire, where
they were used
boldly en masse.

57

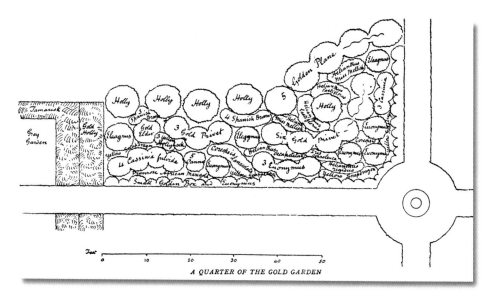

A QUARTER OF THE GOLD GARDEN

Mixed borders and striking single-colour schemes. Miss Jekyll's gold border, mixing types of plants including shrubs, annuals, and hardy and tender perennials (*Colour in the Flower Garden*, 1908).

all giving the impression of growing naturally, and producing the effect of a happy and contented companionship.' The charm of a well-planted hardy flower border, she believed, assumed a delightful informality, but within a definite orderliness in grouping.

Borders were not always limited to particular types of plants, and to provide variety throughout the year contained mixed shrubs, annuals and perennials. This was a particular feature of Miss Jekyll's schemes. Colour schemes might include vibrant colours as long as they were used 'tastefully', a euphemism for 'in moderation'.

Topiary was perhaps the most memorable trademark of Arts and Crafts gardens, with countless shapes and compositions, clipped generally in yew. Topiary was a hangover from manor gardens. The dense population of pieces at Levens Hall had survived all fashion coups since the height of its modishness in the early eighteenth century, although the specimens were replanted over the centuries. By the late nineteenth century this vision of massed specimens in a formal garden setting around the romantic ancient Westmorland hall was particularly evocative for Arts and Crafts followers, and one redolent of the patina of age.

In Arts and Crafts gardens topiary specimens were often restricted to perching atop hedges, in true cottage garden style, although here they lent themselves to a rhythmic repetition. Freestanding specimens, in lines or regularly spaced around terraces, were also popular if garden staffing levels permitted. Occasionally a rival to the over-populated Levens crowd was produced, such as at Heslington Hall, near York. At Earlshall, Fife, Lorimer

imported mature specimens from a derelict garden in Edinburgh. But this magnitude relied on the owner's wealth to employ numerous gardeners to clip the specimens regularly; otherwise they quickly lost their personalities.

Topiary subjects included chess pieces, animals and birds, particularly doves and peacocks, or simpler abstract shapes. These were regarded as indigenous forms, which contrasted with the High Victorian avenues of needle-like Irish yew emulating the Italian cypresses of Renaissance princes. As with hedges, native yew was the favourite material, for its combination of dense, smooth, dark green finish and its relatively quick growth into a recognisable specimen. Vita Sackville-West approved of the topiary at Hidcote, which, she said, was in the 'country tradition' and included 'smug broody hens, bumpy doves and coy peacocks twisting a fat neck towards a fatter tail'.

Another native, box, ran second to yew but was a slower grower. Both were good subjects for complex figures. Other species, such as Portugal laurel, myrtle and holly, were less malleable and smoothly surfaced, and were used for simple shapes. All, however, without regular and brutal maintenance, quickly got out of hand and lost the detail, often becoming merely large, curvaceous blobs, out of scale with their garden surroundings.

Topiary was an essential and prestigious garden feature, redolent of historic manor houses and cottage gardens. At Earlshall, Fife, Lorimer used mature specimens dug up from an Edinburgh garden.

Trees, particularly lime or beech, were pleached, recalling the medieval fashion. The branches were intertwined and pruned regularly above smooth trunks to form an elevated two-dimensional screen, similar to a stilt hedge. They could be used as a single line alongside a path or in pairs to frame the view along the path or vista, as at Sissinghurst in the Lime Walk.

Roses represented medieval romance in the garden, often corralled as bushes in formal beds in the lawns of surprisingly unimaginative and sterile rose gardens. The Arts and Crafts gardener excelled when allowed to liberate roses, using them more freely and imaginatively as specimens, trained up pergolas, mixed with other climbers, or up frames or swagged ropes on poles in lawns or borders. In *Colour in the Flower Garden* (1908) Miss Jekyll recommended bush roses, and 'the kinds of special charm' such as Damask, Provence, Moss and China (now referred to as 'old-fashioned roses'). She also advised using 'those that most nearly concern the garden for beauty and pictorial effect': the rambling and climbing roses that flowered in clusters. She ran ramblers up yew and holly trees 'in regions where the garden joins hands with woodland', and recommended their great usefulness for forming lines of arch and garland as an enclosure to some definite space. Sir George Sitwell,

A crisply shaped peacock, a seminal bird for the Arts and Crafts Movement. Topiary quickly loses its shape if not frequently clipped. Rodmarton, Gloucestershire.

a client of Miss Jekyll's in 1910, was determinedly
lyrical about which types to use (*On the Making of
Gardens*, 1909):

> If it is to be a rose-garden, do not choose those
> stunted, unnatural earth-loving strains, which have
> nothing of vigour or wildness in them ... Let
> climbing roses drop in a veil from the terrace
> and smother with flower-spangled embroidery the
> garden walls, run riot over vaulted arcades, clamber
> up lofty obelisks ...

It was not, however, until the 1930s, with the
advent of Vita Sackville-West's Sissinghurst Castle
Garden, Kent, that 'old-fashioned' roses started to
reclaim their popularity from Tea Roses. Here she
embodied Sir George's advice in the old orchard,
whose trees she smothered in ramblers.

    Climbers, including roses, were planted against
the house, on pergolas or up trees to create romantic bowers. The more
flexible climbers such as rambling roses, clematis, vines (productive and
ornamental) and honeysuckle were suitable for pergolas and to ramp
up trees. The thuggish Russian Vine was popular, having been recently
introduced. Stiffer plants were suitable against the house, with plants of
dubious hardiness that needed shelter, including half-hardy climbers such as
Morning Glory. *Magnolia grandiflora* was a status symbol, with its huge
evergreen leaves and flowers seen from the bedroom windows, but it was
inclined to get out of control and cover paths and windows if not strictly
pruned. Miss Jekyll had equally vigorous vines and figs on her south and
west-facing walls at Munstead Wood, with tender China roses up warm
corners and *Clematis montana* (because it was one of the few clematis varieties
tolerant of Surrey acid soil) on cooler walls. She recommended the purple
Solanum crispum and the tender white *Solanum jasminoides* as beautiful for walls
and for 'free rambling over other wall-growths', and for its long flowering
season from the middle of summer.

Free-form
rose specimens
liberated from
mundane rose
gardens to
pergolas, frames
and old trees in
lawns and orchards
(Samuel Elgood).

    Other specialist gardens included rock gardens, or even Shakespeare or
Tennyson gardens containing flowers referred to by those authors. The great
thing about the compartmentalised garden was that areas at their peak of
flowering at a particular time could remain unseen out of season.

    Pots, tubs and troughs gave terraces an extra dimension of height. Pots
were filled with the sort of architectural foliage plants recommended by
Miss Jekyll, such as hostas, bergenias and ferns. These contrasted with the

GERTRUDE JEKYLL

Gertrude Jekyll (1843–1932) continues to be one of the most influential of all English garden designers, even though many gardeners may hardly have heard of her. Although she was a trained and talented painter and craftswoman from a fairly wealthy family, her passion for gardening began early on at the South Kensington School of Art. She was one of the first designers to take into account the colour, texture, and experience of gardens in influencing design. Her theories on designing with colour were influenced by the painters J. M. W. Turner and Hercules Brabazon Brabazon, by Impressionism, and by the theoretical colour wheel. Her outstanding designs used a subtle, painterly approach to planting, particularly in her hardy flower borders, with radiant colour and the brush-like strokes of her schemes; the Impressionistic-style schemes may have been due to her progressively myopic eyesight, which largely ended her work as a painter, interior designer and craftswoman. In her designs and in works such as the most famous of her many books, *Colour in the Flower Garden* (1908), she used colour harmony through borders. Her most famous combination is the gradual range from 'cool' to 'hot' colours and back again, a technique which continues to be used in garden design today. She was not afraid to use the hot colours of seasonal bedding plants but tempered the eye-catching colours with the irregular shapes of the drifts, and by combining the plants with more neutral or cooler-coloured subjects and backgrounds, using colour harmonies and contrasts which she had worked out and published in 1883 in Robinson's *The English Flower Garden*.

Surprisingly 'hot' colours were used by Miss Jekyll between subtler shades: flaming orange against a calm grey dry-stone wall at Hestercombe, Somerset.

flowers and form of bulbs, particularly lilies, and tender plants such as cannas and geraniums (*Pelargonium*) overwintered and allowed to grow into shrubs, with interesting leaf forms and subtle flower colours. Hydrangeas were a particular favourite of hers in pots. Tubs were for tender, larger, shrubby specimens and topiary; troughs were for smaller subjects, often the newly popular alpines popularised by Reginald Farrer and others, which needed close attention, and whose beauty could be examined in more detail when raised nearer the eye.

The woodland garden was the natural extension of Robinson's *Wild Garden*, and a favourite of Gertrude Jekyll. A woodland canopy beyond the formal garden, preferably of existing native oak, was underplanted with

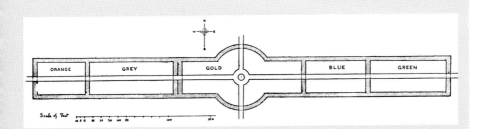

ORANGE GREY GOLD BLUE GREEN

Scale of Feet

A prolific designer from her thirties to the end of her life, she contributed planting plans to over four hundred gardens in the United Kingdom, Europe and the United States. Although her most successful and prolific partnership was with Lutyens, she collaborated with other architects, sometimes on several commissions, including Sidney H. Barnsley at Combend Manor, Gloucestershire (1925); Percy H. Adams at the King Edward VII Sanatorium, Midhurst, West Sussex (1907); Hugh Thackeray Turner, for the Borough of Godalming on the Phillips Memorial at Godalming, Surrey (1912–14); and L. Rome Guthrie for Lord Swaythling at Townhill Park at Bitterne, Hampshire (1912). One of her most successful solo schemes was at the restored Upton Grey Manor House, near Basingstoke (1908–9).

Miss Jekyll's 'special colour garden plan' showing a progression of colours through the border. *Colour in the Flower Garden* (1908).

The Arts and Crafts style was employed for many memorials and memorial gardens, particularly after the First World War, when Miss Jekyll provided a number of schemes, and also for War Grave Cemeteries, of which Lutyens designed 128. She also conceived the idea that the planting for each War Grave headstone should bring the flowers of home to a foreign field, representing the most familiar flowers of English gardens: roses and herbaceous plants, particularly foxgloves, columbines, London pride, nepeta and bergenias. Many of the myriad war grave cemeteries in northern Europe were laid out with Arts and Crafts-inspired buildings in the 1920s.

choice flowering shrubs in drifts with native woodland self-seeders and bulbs. This was all the better if the soil was acid, for precious Far-Eastern introductions that were flooding in, such as camellias, rhododendrons, azaleas, magnolias and other calcifuge plants, could thrive in the correct soil and semi-shaded conditions, along with bulbs such as lilies, the most prized of which was the *Cardiocrinum giganteum*, and gems such as the vivid blue Himalayan poppy (*Meconopsis betonicifolia*). Owners with nothing but thin chalk were doomed to less prized plants unless they could fill large holes with peat and leaf mould, but even then they were unlikely to succeed. Winding grass paths led between the shrub drifts, perhaps to an unexpected and dramatic view of the surrounding countryside.

As with other gardens, lawns were essential, and fine lawns formed a particularly British matrix for these schemes: a restful, well-manicured verdure setting off dark green hedges and topiary, and colourful floral displays. Formal lawns emphasised the architectural setting of the house and garden buildings, while more informal grassed areas merged the garden, as Mawson put it, 'by easy gradation into the landscape beyond', its soft flowing lines respecting the natural contours of the site.

Sporting lawns continued to be important with the traditional bowling green of Drake joined by the recently popular introductions of croquet and, for the more energetic, tennis lawns. Tennis lawns were demanding: initially they required space (some 50 feet by 100 feet), then the expense of good construction, drainage and a boundary fence or hedge, the paraphernalia of nets and posts, and ideally a small pavilion. Such was the popularity of the sport and its social life that most quite modest houses with more than just a back garden boasted at least one tennis court.

Traditional country house features such as kitchen gardens, orchards and parkland were provided where space and funds permitted. Arts and Crafts houses built for holiday use did not always need kitchen gardens, but elsewhere many were laid out such as at Rodmarton, Gloucestershire. Fruit and orchards had a special resonance for the movement and were particularly valued. Space was usually found for a few fruit trees even if a true orchard could not be accommodated. Best of all, when a new house was being built was if it could be sited within part of an old orchard, keeping

Graythwaite, Cumbria (1889), one of Thomas Mawson's first major gardens, which was planted mainly with flowering shrubs (1940s view).

as many old trees as possible, as William Morris and Webb had at Red House in 1859. At Deanery Garden, Berkshire, Lutyens sited Edward Hudson's new house in part of another orchard some forty years later. Part of the orchard was kept alongside Miss Jekyll's planting in Lutyens's layout. Few parks were created from scratch but modest parks surrounded some houses such as Lawrence Johnston's paddocks on the Cotswold scarp at Hidcote, and Mawson's park at Blackwell, Cumbria, framing sweeping views down to Windermere.

At Sissinghurst Castle, Kent, Vita Sackville-West's planting was lavishly developed in the same spirit after her death, until the 1980s, by her brilliant head gardeners Pam Schwerdt and Sibylle Kreutzberger.

FLOWERS·FROM· ❧ ·❧
SHAKESPEARE'S·GARDEN:
a Posy from the Plays, pictured by Walter Crane ❧

Cassell & Co: Lᵈ ❧ 1906 ❧

POPULARISING THE IDEALS: BOOKS, IMAGES, EDUCATION

Arts and crafts gardens were represented in numerous books and paintings, which were romantically attractive and widely disseminated. These images followed the lead of artists such as Helen Allingham and Kate Greenaway who romanticised the 'rural idyll', and the less well known, such as T. H. Hunn. The attractiveness and humanity of the results ensured their continuing popularity.

The more lavish illustrations of bursting borders showcased artists who specialised in painting gardens, including Beatrice Parsons (1870–1955), Samuel Elgood (1851–1943), and Alfred Parsons (1847–1920), and graced books and art and design periodicals. These included Elgood and Jekyll's *Some English Gardens* (1904) and, from 1893, *The Studio*, an art and design periodical founded and edited by Charles Holme, who lived in Morris's Red House and owned Upton Grey Manor House, Hampshire. Three editions of *The Studio* in 1907, 1908 and 1911 illustrated gardens throughout Britain in photographs, but these were interspersed with colour reproductions of romantic watercolours by Elgood and others, depicting the Arts and Crafts style of planting. Ernest Chadwick (1876–1955) provided a significant number of illustrations for Mawson – many being used in the fourth (1912) and fifth (1926) editions of *The Art and Craft of Garden Making*. Chadwick was a Birmingham artist of some renown specialising in rural scenes, landscapes and gardens.

The best garden photographs appeared in *Country Life Illustrated*, with high-quality and beautifully composed black-and-white shots of houses and gardens, in a glossy magazine which positively promoted the Arts and Crafts philosophy and depicted many of its newly built houses and gardens. *Country Life* was owned and published by Edward Hudson, a self-made man for whom Lutyens and Jekyll produced so many designs. Hudson commissioned the golden pair to create homes and gardens for himself, including the rugged and remote Lindisfarne Castle on Holy Island, Northumberland (1911), an aspiring Home Counties manor house in a former orchard at Deanery Garden, Berkshire (1899–1901), and also Plumpton Place, East Sussex.

Opposite:
Books and paintings represented Arts and Crafts gardens as romantically attractive and were widely disseminated. Walter Crane, frontispiece, *Flowers from Shakespeare's Garden* (1906).

67

The finest of garden photographs appeared weekly from 1897 in the ultimate in aspirational lifestyle periodicals, *Country Life Illustrated*. Owner and proprietor Edward Hudson lived the ideal in his four Lutyens houses, whose gardens had Jekyll planting. Deanery Garden, Berkshire.

The bindings of garden books were finely designed and crafted in true Arts and Crafts spirit. Beatrice Parsons and E. T. Cook's *Gardens of England* (1908) contains Parsons' romantic views of gardens planted in the Arts and Crafts style.

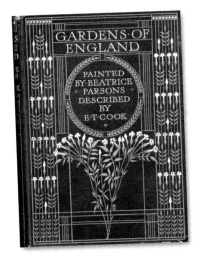

Miss Jekyll illustrated her numerous garden books (some of which remain in print today) lavishly with photographs; most of these, including *Garden Ornament* (1918) and *Gardens for Small Country Houses* (1912), were published by *Country Life*. Other authors used engravings and line drawings to illustrate their manuals of design, including plantsman William Robinson (*The English Flower Garden*, 1883, numerous later editions and in print today), landscape architect Thomas Mawson (*The Art and Craft of Garden Making*), and architects Baillie Scott (*Houses and Gardens*, 1906), Sedding (*Garden-Craft Old and New*, 1891), Blomfield (*The Formal Garden in England*, 1892) and Godfrey (*Gardens in the Making*, 1914). The bird's-eye view was especially suited to this treatment, echoing the well-known set of country house illustrations by Knyff and Kip in the late seventeenth and early eighteenth centuries. Baillie Scott included colour reproductions of his own beautiful watercolours.

Even the bindings of these publications were finely designed, detailed and tooled in true Arts and Crafts spirit. One of the finest is Beatrice Parsons and E. T. Cook's *Gardens of England* (1908) with its beautifully coloured and tooled binding, also *Scottish Gardens: Being a Representative Selection of Different Types, Old and New*, written by Sir Herbert Maxwell and illustrated by Mary Wilson (1908). More modest books had illustrated bindings, including Violet Biddle's *Small Gardens* (c. 1903). Even catalogues had attractively designed covers, such as John P. White's garden furniture catalogue of the Pyghtle Works, Bedford, and Harwood of Balham's seed catalogue.

The Arts and Crafts movement and publications by its followers did much to encourage the popularity of gardening in this style as a hobby, which has continued to the present day. On 25 November 1871 William Robinson founded the

Garden catalogues had lavishly designed covers to entice aspiring purchasers, such as John P. White's Pyghtle Works furniture catalogue, Bedford.

Even the humble seed catalogue might be artistically covered: Harwood of Balham, 1895.

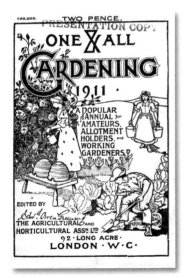

Far left: Ephemeral literature was informative and helped to educate gardeners of modest means.

Left: Some horticultural prizes were prestigious enough to warrant high artistic quality and craftsmanship. Plaque by the sculptor Hamo Thorneycroft, donated by seedsmen Toogoods, 1919.

weekly magazine *The Garden*, to which Ruskin contributed frequently and Morris occasionally. Miss Jekyll wrote numerous pieces from 1881, becoming joint editor with E. T. Cook for two years in 1900 and 1901. Ephemeral literature appeared, including manuals and catalogues. Amateur horticultural clubs for the public were founded and spawned flower shows, where gardeners could show off their horticultural prowess. Horticultural competitions needed prizes and some were of high artistic quality and craftsmanship.

LADY GARDENERS

Professional horticulture became acceptable for women. Education was necessary and several ladies' gardening colleges appeared, such as the Glynde College for Lady Gardeners and Studley College for Ladies. Indeed, of the Glynde College it was noted in 1906 in *The Bystander* magazine:

> Every form of gardening can be studied at Glynde; digging, hoeing, treatment of seedlings and greenhouse plants, the care of lawns, paths, and beds, in fact, every branch of the science, for the highest technical skill is required to make gardening a paying concern.

The Gardening College, Glynde, East Sussex (founded 1902). *The Bystander* reported in 1906, 'Many ladies, through necessity, have to earn their own livelihood, and one of the most attractive ways of doing so, as well as one in which the competition is not severe, is that of gardening.'

Miss Jekyll fully approved of this, being a hands-on gardener herself, and in 1907 'lady gardeners' carried out her planting schemes at the recently built King Edward VII Sanatorium, a private tuberculosis sanatorium near Midhurst, West Sussex. Margaret Biddulph trained as a horticulturist at Studley College before she employed William Scrubey (whom she had met there) as head gardener at Rodmarton, where he designed the planting within Ernest Barnsley's framework. The Women's Farm and Garden Union was founded in 1899, of which Miss Jekyll became one of the vice-presidents in 1916.

FURTHER READING

BOOKS

Baillie Scott. *Houses and Gardens: Arts and Crafts Interiors*.
Antique Collectors' Club, 1995 (first published 1906).

Baker, Derek. *The Flowers of William Morris*. Barn Elms, 1996.

Barker, M. *Edwin Lutyens*. Shire, 2005.

Bisgrove, R. *Gertrude Jekyll's Colour Schemes for the Flower Garden*.
Frances Lincoln, 1988.

Bisgrove, R. *The Gardens of Gertrude Jekyll*. Frances Lincoln, 1992.

Blomfield, R., and Thomas, I. *The Formal Garden in England*.
Waterstone, 1985 (first published 1892).

Brown, J. *Gardens of a Golden Afternoon – The Story of a Partnership:
Edwin Lutyens and Gertrude Jekyll*. Allen Lane, 1982.

Davey, P. *Arts and Crafts Architecture*. Phaidon, 1995.

Greenstead, M. *The Arts and Crafts Movement in Britain*. Shire, 2010.

Haywood, A. *Norah Lindsay: The Life and Art of a Garden Designer*.
Frances Lincoln, 2007.

Hitchmough, W. *Arts and Crafts Gardens*. Pavilion Books, 1997.

Hitchmough, W. *Arts and Crafts Gardens*. V&A Publications, 2005.

Jekyll, G. *Colour Schemes for the Flower Garden*. Antique Collectors' Club,
as *Colour in the Flower Garden*, 1982 (first published 1908).

Jekyll, G. *Garden Ornament*. Antique Collectors' Club, 1982
(first published 1918).

Miller, M. *English Garden Cities: An Introduction*. English Heritage, 2010.

Mowl, T. *Historic Gardens of Gloucestershire*. Tempus, 2002.

Muthesius, H. *The English House*. English translation of 1904,
Frances Lincoln, 2007.

Ottewill, D. *The Edwardian Garden*. Yale University Press, 1989.

Peto, Harold A. (editor R. Whalley). *The Boke of Iford*. Libanus Press,
1993 (first published 1917).

Pevsner, N. *Pevsner's Architectural Glossary*. Yale University Press, 2010.

Robinson, W. *The English Flower Garden*. Murray, 1883 and later editions.

Sullivan, S. *Phillips Memorial Park: An Arts and Crafts Movement Tribute to
a Hero of the Titanic*. The Society for the Arts and Crafts Movement
in Surrey, 2012.

Symes, M. *A Glossary of Garden History*. Shire, second edition 2006.

Tankard, J. *Gardens of the Arts and Crafts Movement*. Harry N. Abrahams, 2004.

Tankard, J. *Gertrude Jekyll and the Country House Garden: From the Archives of
Country Life*. Aurum Press, 2011.

Tankard, J., and Wood, M. A. *Gertrude Jekyll at Munstead Wood: Writing,
Horticulture, Photography, Homebuilding*. Bramley Books, 1998.

Tooley, M., and Arnander, P. *Gertrude Jekyll: Essays on the Life of a Working Amateur*. Michaelmas Books, 1995.

Way, T. *Gertrude Jekyll*. Shire, 2012.

Weaver, L. *Houses and Gardens by E. L. Lutyens*. Antique Collectors' Club, 1998 (first published 1913).

Whalley, R. *The Great Edwardian Gardens of Harold Peto: From the Archives of Country Life*. Aurum Press, 2007.

WEBSITES
See Places to Visit, below, for web addresses of individual sites.

Association of Gardens Trusts: www.gardenstrusts.org.uk
Garden History Society: www.gardenhistorysociety.org.uk
Images of England (listed buildings): www.imagesofengland.org.uk
Lutyens Trust: www.lutyenstrust.org.uk
Society for the Arts and Crafts Movement in Surrey:
    www.artsandcraftsmovementinsurrey.org.uk
UK Parks and Gardens Database: www.parksandgardens.ac.uk
Voysey Commissions and Other Aspects of His Career:
    www.voysey.gotik-romanik.de
Voysey Society: www.voyseysociety.com

APPENDIX: DESIGNERS AND THEIR BEST WORKS

The best British Arts and Crafts gardens were scattered across England, Scotland and Wales. In England regional hotspots occurred in Surrey (the original epicentre), the Cotswolds (which succeeded Surrey, with contrasting concentrations around Broadway and Sapperton), Sussex, the Southwest, East Anglia and the Lake District.

Key examples of designers' garden work are as follows:

BAILLIE SCOTT, MACKAY HUGH (1865–1945)
Blackwell, Windermere, Cumbria (*c.* 1900) with Thomas Mawson
Snowshill, Broadway, Gloucestershire (1919–23), plan adapted by owner
    Charles Wade

BARNSLEY, ERNEST (1863–1926)
Upper Dorvel House, Sapperton, Gloucestershire (from 1901),
  architect's own house
Rodmarton Manor, near Cirencester, Gloucestershire (1909–29),
  with William Scrubey, Head Gardener

BLOMFIELD, REGINALD (1856–1942)
Godinton Park, Kent (1902)

BLOW, DETMAR (1867–1939)
Happisburgh Manor, Norfolk (1900)

DILLISTONE, GEORGE (1877–1957)
Castle Drogo, Devon (c. 1922), with Lutyens
Goddards, York (late 1920s)
Markyatecell Park, Hertfordshire (c. 1910)

JEKYLL, GERTRUDE (1843–1932)
Munstead, Surrey (1878)
Upton Grey Manor, Basingstoke, Hampshire (1908–9)
Vann, Surrey (1911)
Mount Stewart, Newtownards, Co. Down, Northern Ireland
  (1920, the Sunken Garden)
Redcliffe, Whittingehame, East Lothian, Scotland (1925)
Bonaly Tower, Colinton, Edinburgh, Scotland (1926)

LINDSAY, NORAH (1873–1948)
Sutton Courtenay, Oxfordshire (1900 onwards)
Blickling Hall, Norfolk (1920s–30s)
Cliveden, Buckinghamshire (1920s–30s)
Port Lympne, Kent (1920s)
Trent Park, Middlesex (1924–6)
Hidcote, Gloucestershire (1930s)

LORIMER, ROBERT (1864–1929)
Kellie Castle, Fife (1880s)
Earlshall, Leuchars, Fife (1890s)
High Barn, Surrey (1901–3)
Brackenburgh, Cumbria (1903–4)
Hill of Tarvit, Cupar, Fife (1906–7)
Lympne Castle, Kent (1907–9)
Formakin, Renfrewshire (1908, pre-dating the new house)

LUTYENS, EDWIN (1869–1944), AND JEKYLL, GERTRUDE

Munstead Wood, Godalming, Surrey (from 1883), Miss Jekyll's own house
Orchards, Busbridge, Surrey (1897–1902), their most important
    early work
Goddards, Abinger Common, Surrey (1898–1900)
Deanery Garden, Sonning, Berkshire (1899–1901),
    for *Country Life* owner Edward Hudson
Marsh Court, Hampshire (1901–4)
Hestercombe, Taunton, Somerset (1903–9)
Folly Farm, Sulhamstead, Berkshire (1906 and 1912)
Heywood, Abbeyleix, Ireland (1910)

MALLOWS, CHARLES EDWARD (1864–1915)

Tirley Garth, Tarporley Cheshire (1906–12), with Thomas Mawson
Craig-y-Parc, Pentyrch, Cardiff, Glamorgan (1913–15)

MAWSON, THOMAS (1861–1933)

Graythwaite Hall, Ulverston, Cumbria (1889)
Brockhole, Windermere, Cumbria (1899) with architect Dan Gibson
Wood, Devon (*c.* 1904), with Dan Gibson
Roynton Cottage, Rivington, Lancashire (from 1906)
Dyffryn, St Nicholas, Vale of Glamorgan (from 1906)

PARSONS, ALFRED (1847–1920)

Wightwick Manor, near Wolverhampton (*c.* 1890)

PRIOR, E. S. (1852–1932)

The Barn, Exmouth, Devon (1896–7)
Home Place (now Voewood), Holt, Norfolk (1903–6)

SCHULTZ, ROBERT WEIR (1860–1951)

Old Place of Mochrum, Wigtownshire (1903)

THOMAS, F. INIGO (1865–1950)

Athelhampton, near Dorchester (1891–3)

TIPPING, H. AVRAY (1855–1933)

Mathern Palace, near Chepstow, Monmouthshire (from 1894)
Mounton House, near Chepstow, Monmouthshire (from 1911)
High Glanau, Lydart (from 1923), architect's own house

TRIGGS, H. INIGO (1876—1923)
Little Boarhunt, Liphook, Hampshire (1910–11), architect's own house

TURNER, HUGH THACKERAY (1853—1937)
Westbrook, Godalming, Surrey (1899), architect's own house
Phillips Memorial, Godalming, Surrey (1913), with Gertrude Jekyll

VOYSEY, CHARLES (1857—1941)
New Place, Haslemere, Surrey (1897–1901)

WEBB, PHILIP SPEAKMAN (1831—1915)
Red House, Bexleyheath, Kent (1859), for William Morris
Great Tangley Manor, Surrey (c. 1885)

WILLIAMS-ELLIS, CLOUGH (1883—1978)
Plas Brondanw, Tremadoc, Gwynedd (from 1908), architect's own house
Cornwell Manor and village, Oxfordshire (1939)

Amateur designers were also important. Their greatest creations include:

Hidcote Manor, Gloucestershire (from 1907),
   by Lawrence Johnston (1871–1958)
Kiftsgate, near Hidcote, Gloucestershire (from 1917),
   by Mrs Heather Muir with Lawrence Johnston
Parcevall Hall, near Skipton, North Yorkshire (1927–60),
   by Sir William Milner (1893–1960), 8th Baronet of Nun Appleton
Sissinghurst, Kent (1930s–1940s),
   by Vita Sackville-West (1892–1962) and Harold Nicolson (1886–1968)
St Nicholas, Richmond, North Yorkshire (1905–25),
   by the Honourable Robert (Bobbie) James (1873–1960)

PLACES TO VISIT

Most of the following gardens open to the public are mentioned in the text.
Some are open only by appointment or at limited times.
Please check the website before travelling.

GARDENS

SOUTH

The Barn Hotel, Foxholes Hill, Exmouth, Devon EX8 2DF
(open by appointment or by staying at the hotel).
Telephone: 01395 224411. Website: www.barnhotel.co.uk

Castle Drogo, Drewsteignton, Exeter, Devon EX6 6PB. Telephone: 01647
433306. Website: www.nationaltrust.org.uk/castle-drogo

Coleton Fishacre, Brownstone Road, Kingswear, Devon TQ6 0EQ.
Telephone: 01803 752466.
Website: www.nationaltrust.org.uk/coleton-fishacre

Compton Cemetery and Watts Mortuary Chapel, Compton, Godalming, Surrey.
Website: www.wattsgallery.org.uk

Goddards, Abinger Common, Surrey. Telephone: 01628 825920.
Website: www.landmarktrust.org.uk

Hestercombe Gardens, Cheddon Fitzpaine, Taunton, Somerset TA2 8LG.
Telephone: 01823 413923. Website: www.hestercombe.com

Iford Manor, Bradford-on-Avon, Wiltshire BA15 2BA.
Telephone: 01225 863146. Website: www.ifordmanor.co.uk.

Kelmscott Manor, Kelmscott, Lechlade, Gloucestershire GL7 3HJ.
Telephone: 01367 253348. Website: www.kelmscottmanor.co.uk

Lytes Cary Manor, near Somerton, Somerset TA11 7HU. Telephone: 01458
224471. Website: www.nationaltrust.org.uk/lytes-cary-manor

The Manor House, Upton Grey, Hampshire RG25 2RD.
Telephone: 01256 862827. Website: www.gertrudejekyllgarden.co.uk

The Pergola and Hill Garden, Hampstead, London NW3 7EX
(entrance on Inverforth Close, off North End Way).
Website: www.hampsteadheath.net/historical

Phillips Memorial Park and Cloister, Godalming, Surrey.
Website: www.waverley.gov.uk/info/670/parks_and_open_
spaces-outdoor_facilities/740/phillips_memorial_park_and_
cloister_ godalming

Postman Park, Edward Street, London EC1A 7BX.
Website: www.wattsgallery.org.uk

Red House, Red House Lane, Bexleyheath, London DA6 8JF.
Telephone: 0208 304 9878. Website: www.nationaltrust.org.uk/redhouse

The Salutation, Knightrider Street, Sandwich, Kent CT13 9EW.
  Telephone: 01304 619919. Website: www.the-secretgardens.co.uk
Sissinghurst Castle, Cranbrook, Kent TN17 2AB. Telephone: 01580 710700.
  Website: www.nationaltrust.org.uk/sissinghurst-castle
Standen, West Hoathly Road, East Grinstead, West Sussex RH19 4NE.
  Telephone: 01342 323029. Website: www.nationaltrust.org.uk/standen
Vann, Hambledon, Godalming, Surrey GU8 4EF.
  Telephone: 01428 683413. Website: www.vanngarden.co.uk

MIDLANDS & EAST ANGLIA
Hidcote Manor, Hidcote Bartrim, Chipping Campden, Gloucestershire
  GL55 6LR. Telephone: 01386 438333.
  Website: www.nationaltrust.org.uk/hidcote
Kiftsgate Court, Chipping Campden, Gloucestershire GL55 6LN.
  Telephone: 01386 438777. Website: www.kiftsgate.co.uk
Misarden Park Gardens, Miserden, Stroud, Gloucestershire GL6 7JA.
  Telephone: 01285 821303. Website: www.misardenpark.co.uk
Owlpen Manor, Dursley, Gloucestershire GL11 5BZ.
  Telephone: 01453 860 261. Website: www.owlpen.com
The Pleasaunce Christian Endeavour Holiday Centre, Harbord Road,
  Overstrand, near Cromer, Norfolk NR27 0PN.
  Telephone: 01263 579212. Website: www.pleasaunce.co.uk
Rodmarton Manor, Cirencester, Gloucestershire GL7 6PF.
  Telephone: 01285 841253. Website: www.rodmarton-manor.co.uk
Snowshill Manor, near Broadway, Worcestershire WR12 7JU. Telephone:
  01386 842814. Website: www.nationaltrust.org.uk/snowshill-manor
Voewood, Cromer Road, High Kelling, Norfolk NR25 6QS.
  Telephone: 01263 713029. Website: www.voewood.com
Wightwick Manor, Wightwick Bank, Wolverhampton WV6 8EE.
  Telephone: 01902 760100.
  Website: www.nationaltrust.org.uk/wightwick-manor

NORTH
Blackwell Museum, Bowness-on-Windermere, Cumbria LA23 3JT.
  Telephone: 01539 446139. Website: www.blackwell.org.uk
Brantwood, Coniston, Cumbria LA21 8AD.
  Telephone: 01539 441396. Website: www.brantwood.org.uk
Brockhole, The Lake District Visitor Centre, Windermere, Cumbria LA23 1LJ.
  Telephone: 01539 446601. Website: www.brockhole.co.uk
Goddards, 27 Tadcaster Road, Dringhouses, York, North Yorkshire YO24 1GG.
  Telephone: 01904 702021.
  Website: www.nationaltrust.org.uk/goddards

Graythwaite Hall, Graythwaite, Ulverston, Cumbria LA12 8BA.
Telephone: 01539 531333. Website: www.graythwaitehall.co.uk
Parcevall Hall Gardens, Skyreholme, Skipton, North Yorkshire BD23 6DE.
Telephone: 01756 720311. Website: www.parcevallhallgardens.co.uk

WALES
Dyffryn Gardens, Duffryn Lane, St Nicholas, Vale of Glamorgan CF5 6SU.
Telephone: 029 2059 3328. Website: www.dyffryngardens.org.uk
Plas Brondanw Gardens, Llanfrothen, Gwynedd LL48 6SW.
Telephone: 01766 772772. Website: www.brondanw.org

SCOTLAND
Crathes Castle Garden, Crathes, Banchory, Aberdeenshire AB31 5QJ.
Telephone: 0845 643 9215.
Website: www.nts.org.uk/property/crathes-castle-garden-estate
Earlshall Castle Gardens, Leuchars, Fife KY16 0DP. Telephone: 01334 839205.
Website: www.welcometoscotland.com/things-to-do/attractions/
gardens-and-nurseries/fife/earlshall-castle-gardens
Greywalls Hotel, Muirfield, Gullane, East Lothian EH31 2EG
(open by visiting the hotel as a guest). Telephone: 01620 842144.
Website: www.greywalls.co.uk
Hill of Tarvit Mansionhouse and Garden, Cupar, Fife KY15 5PB.
Telephone: 0844 493 2185. Website: www.nts.org.uk/Property/
Hill-of-Tarvit-Mansionhouse-Garden
Kellie Castle and Garden, Pittenweem, Fife KY10 2RF. Telephone: 0844 493
2184. Website: www.nts.org.uk/Property/Kellie-Castle-Garden

FRANCE
Le Bois des Moutiers, France, Route de l'Eglise 76119, Varengeville-sur-Mer.
Telephone: 02 35 85 10 02.
Website: www.boisdesmoutiers.com

GARDEN CITIES AND MODEL VILLAGES
Bournville Village Trust, Birmingham.
Telephone: 0121 472 3831. Website: www.bvt.org.uk
Hampstead Garden Suburb, London.
Telephone: 020 8455 7410. Website: www.hgs.org.uk
Letchworth Garden City. Telephone: 01462 476007 (Heritage Foundation).
Website: www.letchworth.com
New Earswick, York, North Yorkshire.
Port Sunlight, near Birkenhead, Merseyside. Telephone: 0151 644 6466
(Port Sunlight Museum). Website: www.portsunlightvillage.com

Oppostie:
Hidcote Manor,
Gloucestershire,
a masterpiece
by its owner,
Lawrence
Johnstone. It
was laid out from
1907 to the 1920s.

INDEX

Page numbers in italics refer to
illustrations